Learning About
Hidden Treasure

by Lucy Townsend
illustrated by Lydia Halverson

 CHILDRENS PRESS, CHICAGO

Library of Congress Cataloging in Publication Data

Townsend, Lucy.
  Learning about hidden treasure.

  (The Learning about series)
  Summary: Relates the stories of many hidden treasures,
some discovered and some still undiscovered, from the
lost wealth of Captain Kidd to recently found sunken
galleons off the coast of Florida.
    1. Treasure-trove—Juvenile literature.
[1. Buried treasure]   I. Halverson, Lydia, ill.
II. Title.   II. Series.
G525.T586   1987   910.4'53   87-9396
ISBN 0-516-06549-1

Learning About
Hidden Treasure

created by THE CHILD'S WORLD

Suppose you found a treasure map hidden away in your attic. What would you do? Tell all your friends? Put the map back in its hiding place? Grab a shovel and start looking? Think before you answer. Hunting for buried treasure can be very dangerous!

Where do buried treasures come from? Most people think that
they were hidden by pirates. That is sometimes true, of course.
But not always!

Sometimes treasures come from sunken ships. Divers dive to the ocean floor to find them. Sometimes treasures are found on beaches, washed ashore by ocean tides.

Some treasures are found where they were buried during war. And sometimes, treasures are found that were simply hidden away in a safe place and forgotten.

There are some people who would do just about anything to find and keep a famous treasure. So if you should find a hidden treasure or even a treasure map, you would have to be on guard. Hunting for treasure can be serious business!

Long ago, seafaring people realized the risks connected with treasures. So they took care to protect themselves. For example, when one of them hid a treasure, he hid it on a dark night, and he did it alone.

And sometimes in the West Indies, when one hid a treasure, he would first offer a chicken or goat as a sacrifice. He would cut up the animal and pour its blood on the treasure chest. Or he might bury the dead animal along with the treasure.

Pirates followed many rules when they buried loot. Some pirate captains made the crew draw lots. The mate who drew the unlucky lot had to carry the treasure chest to its hiding place and dig the hole. Then the captain would kill the pirate and toss his body on the chest. Some captains sprinkled the dead pirate's blood in the hole. They believed that the ghost of the dead pirate would guard the treasure. Since very few pirate treasures have been found, maybe they were right!

There are rules for digging up a treasure, too.

Seafarers would warn you to search for treasure only at night. And not in the moonlight. The best time to look would be after midnight. The worst thing you could do would be to speak. If you said, "I found it!" or "Wow! Look at this!" the treasure chest would disappear. Or, if the treasure was gold, it would turn to sand.

Most seafarers will tell you that keeping a treasure is much harder than digging it up. That is because many treasures, once found, have been stolen, and sometimes stolen again.

Legend says that if you find a treasure that has been stolen, the spirit of greed will fall on you. To keep from becoming greedy, you can leave part of the treasure behind, or give half of it to someone in need.

If you should find a treasure, what rules would you follow to protect yourself?

OLD PIRATE GOLD

Seafarers love to tell tales about pirate treasures. Maybe you have heard about the stolen gold of

CAPTAIN KIDD.

This sea captain once lived quietly with his wife and children in New York City. But in 1695 he sailed away to capture pirates and, instead, became a pirate himself.

People said that Captain Kidd wrote letters with the blood of his victims. They also said that he buried hundreds of treasure chests full of gold, silver, and precious jewels.

In 1701 Captain Kidd was caught and condemned to die for piracy. He promised to guide his captors to a rich treasure if they let him live. But they wouldn't listen. Captain Kidd died on the gallows, and his treasures remained hidden.

Captain Kidd left a desk and three big chests. Each of these contained a secret place with a treasure map inside. On each map was a drawing of the same island. Many people tried to find the island drawn on these maps. But so far, no one has found Captain Kidd's treasure.

There are many fictional stories based on Captain Kidd's treasure. The best known story is Edgar Allan Poe's

THE GOLD BUG.

This tale is about a man named William Legrand who lived on an island near the coast of South Carolina. His favorite hobby was studying insects. One day he found a strange bug—not a real bug but one made of gold.

On the ground near the bug was a piece of paper. William used this paper to pick up the bug. Later that day, the paper was accidently held near a fire. William saw that the heat from the fire had revealed secret writing. The paper showed a kid, a skull, and a coded message—clues to a hidden treasure.

William broke the code. Then he took a friend and a servant and followed the clues. They led to a skull hidden in the limb of a tree. Following the directions, William tied a string around the golden bug. He told his servant to drop it through the eye socket of the skull. William then measured fifty feet from where the bug dropped. He and his companions dug for almost four hours. Finally they found an old chest. It was filled with gold coins, gold watches, gold ornaments, and diamonds, rubies, emeralds, and sapphires.

William was sure that this was the famous treasure hidden by Captain Kidd.

There are many legends about the treasures of the pirate

JEAN LAFITTE.

This clever Frenchman was a blacksmith in New Orleans in 1809. But he made extra money smuggling. Soon he became a rich pirate.

Jean Lafitte wore fine clothes and ate in the best restaurants of New Orleans. People knew he was a pirate. Once they had him arrested. But Lafitte managed to be acquitted.

Soon afterwards, he decided to move to an island off the Texas coast. Nobody knows what finally happened to him. One day his pirate ship *Pride* simply disappeared.

People around New Orleans say that Jean Lafitte used to fill cannon barrels with gold. Then he would plug the end of each barrel and drop the barrels from his ship into the ocean.

No one knows how the pirate planned to find the barrels again or how he would get them from the bottom of the ocean. Why do you suppose the pirate tossed his gold overboard?

The scariest pirate on the Spanish Main was

BLACKBEARD.

Edward Teach was huge, mean and ugly. He was called Blackbeard because of his long, black beard. People said his voice sounded like a roaring cannon.

When Blackbeard went to battle, he stuck matches in his hat and beard. Whenever he boarded a ship, he set his matches on fire, waved his cutlass, and screamed curses. He was so cruel that people said he must be a child of the Devil.

There are many legends about the treasures that Blackbeard buried along the coast of North America. He often said, "Only the Devil knows where my treasures are buried. Nobody will get them but the Devil or me!"

Many people have hunted for Blackbeard's treasures, but no one has found them. Some people say they belong to the Devil. What do you think?

One legend tells about how Blackbeard's wives got to see

BLACKBEARD'S TREASURE ROOM.

Between voyages, Blackbeard lived in a castle on the island of St. Thomas in the Caribbean Sea. Each of his fourteen wives lived there with him.

When Blackbeard grew tired of a wife, he would guide her down the winding steps of a tower. At the bottom was Blackbeard's treasure room.

In the room were heaps of gold, diamonds, and jewels. In her excitement, the wife would rush over to examine them.

Blackbeard would slam and lock the door. The poor woman would scream and cry, but Blackbeard would only laugh. He knew she would soon die in the locked room.

The treasure story that kids love best is

TREASURE ISLAND

by Robert Louis Stevenson.

Long ago, a boy named Jim Hawkins lived with his parents in the Admiral Benbow Inn. One day a sick seaman named Billy Bones moved into the inn. Later a blind pirate arrived. He scared Billy Bones so badly that Billy had a stroke and died.

Jim then opened a chest belonging to Billy and found a treasure map. He took the map to his neighbors, Dr. Livesey and Squire Trelawney. They hired a ship called the *Hispaniola* and, with Jim, set sail for Treasure Island.

They made a mistake, though, in hiring one-legged Long John Silver to be the ship's cook. Long John was really a pirate in disguise who planned to take over the ship when it got to Treasure Island.

Jim Hawkins helped save his friends from the pirates. He overheard Long John Silver plotting to take over the *Hispaniola*. He warned his friends in time for them to get to safety. Then, after a terrible battle, Jim got the *Hispaniola* back from the pirates.

After these adventures, Jim Hawkins and his friends found the treasure and sailed back to England. Along the way, Long John Silver escaped with one bag of gold.

WELL-GUARDED TREASURES

Seafarers will tell you that most treasures are guarded. Often a ghost hovers nearby. Or it might be a monster or sea creature. Sometimes the treasure is in such a dangerous place that Nature seems to be standing guard over the gold.

If you visit Scotland, you may hear the legend of the ghost that guards the

SPANISH GALLEON OF TOBERMORY.

One day after a terrible storm, a Spanish galleon slipped into a bay in Scotland. Some people said that a Spanish princess was on board the ship and that she carried with her a great treasure of gold.

The Spaniards rowed to shore and asked for food and water. But they soon got into a quarrel with the Scots, and some Spanish sailors were dragged to a dungeon. The Spaniards paid back the Scots by capturing a boy and taking him to their galleon.

The Spaniards decided to sail away, taking the Scottish boy with them. But suddenly their galleon blew up and sank in the harbor. Some people said that witches had blown up the ship. Others said that the Scottish boy had set off the explosion.

The body of the Spanish princess washed up on shore. The Scots quickly buried her, but they say that her ghost still haunts the harbor. Whenever someone takes gold from the wreck, the princess haunts him until he puts the gold back.

Seafarers of Ireland tell a strange tale about the

ROYAL OAK TREASURE.

Long ago, a rich treasure ship named *Royal Oak* was sailing in the ocean near Ireland. A storm forced the ship close to an island. There were no lights on the island to warn the captain of land. So his ship crashed and sank.

Divers were sent to bring up the treasure of the sunken vessel. The divers found the wreck. But they left the treasure there and refused to swim back a second time. People asked the divers what was wrong. But they would not answer.

The people living on the island say that a huge sea serpent is coiled around the sunken wreck. This creature guards the treasure of the *Royal Oak*.

One well-guarded treasure lies in

VIGO BAY.

Long ago, Spanish ships carried precious treasure from the New World back to Spain. Because the Spaniards were afraid of warships from other nations, their ships sailed in fleets.

In 1702, forty, rich, Spanish ships left the New World. They reached the harbor of Vigo, north of Spain. But the English navy heard about the treasure fleet and attacked. Many Spanish ships burned and sank in the harbor.

For over 200 years, treasure-hunters tried to bring up the gold from the sunken ships. They sent down divers. They dragged the bay with hooks. They even blasted the wrecks with dynamite. They still did not find much gold.

What guards this treasure? MUD. Forty feet of it. Imagine trying to pull a treasure out of the thick, gooey muck!

Have you heard the legend of the

DIVINING ROD TREASURE?

According to this legend, a man used a divining rod to search for treasure. On a dark and lonely night, this treasure-hunter walked along, holding his divining rod. Suddenly the rod began to shake. The man put down the rod and began to dig. He dug and dug. At last, he hit a wooden chest. He opened the chest and found heaps of gold and jewels.

Suddenly he heard the flap of a thousand wings. He looked up and saw a flock of birds. Headless birds! The man dropped the gold and ran away as fast as he could. He never went near the treasure again.

UNLUCKY LOOT

Many seafarers will warn you to stay away from buried treasure. After all, they say, the treasure is not yours. It belongs to the person who buried it or to the ghost that guards it. If you do manage to take the treasure away, you will have bad luck. Or so they say.

One bad-luck legend is about the treasure of

TORY ISLAND.

The legend says that a treasure was hidden long ago on Tory Island near a deep hole called Balor's Prison. A giant, named Balor of the Evil Eye, put it there.

According to the legend, a woman and her son visited Tory Island. While they were there, they dug up the treasure. Soon both of them became sick. Doctors were called, but they could not help. Hour after hour the woman and her son grew worse. To save them, the people on the island put the treasure back in its hiding place. From that moment on, the woman and her son began to get well.

No one else has ever tried to dig up the treasure. Would you?

Have you ever visited Padre Island off the coast of Texas? In 1553 a fleet of rich Spanish galleons sank in the waters off the island. Ever since, treasures have washed up on the beach.

One bad-luck tale the people on Padre Island tell is about

JOHN SINGER'S TREASURE.

For many years John Singer lived near the beach on Padre Island. His hobby was searching for treasures. Whenever a storm blew up, he would look for gold coins on the beach. He gathered a large treasure.

One day, during the Civil War, John Singer heard that the Union soldiers were on their way to the island. He did not want them to take away his riches, so he dug a hole six miles from his house and hid the treasure.

After the war was over, Singer wanted to dig for his treasure. But he couldn't remember where he had buried it.

John Singer died without ever finding his treasure. Now that was bad luck!

MYSTERIOUS TREASURES

Some treasures keep people guessing for centuries. There may be several clues. There may even be a treasure map. People look and look. But the treasure remains hidden.

One mystery treasure may be hidden on

OAK ISLAND.

In 1798, sixteen-year-old Daniel McGinnis and his friends visited Oak Island near the coast of Nova Scotia, Canada. They noticed a mysterious tree on the island. The tree looked as though it had been used to support a pulley and rope. Daniel knew that sailors used pulleys and ropes to pick up heavy chests. Maybe a treasure was hidden under the tree.

Daniel and his friends began to dig. Every ten feet they found a wooden platform. They dug and dug. Finally, they got tired and gave up.

Another group of treasure-hunters dug in the same spot. When they reached ninety-five feet, they found a bigger platform. Since night was coming on, they decided to rest. The next morning the hole was full of salt water. No matter how much they bailed, the hole remained full.

For over a hundred years, people searched for the treasure on Oak Island. They discovered a gold chain, a piece of paper, and a slab with mysterious writing on it.

Treasure-hunters finally discovered why the hole keeps filling up with water. Someone had dug two tunnels to the ocean. Water drains from the ocean into the treasure hole. People have tried many times to keep the water from filling the hole. But so far, they have failed.

Treasure-hunters have spent a fortune trying to find the treasure on Oak Island. No one knows if the mysterious treasure will ever be found or if a treasure is there at all. But in 1967, a television camera was sent down. It photographed what looked like three chests and a skeleton's hand. So, treasure-hunters keep trying. Maybe one day the Oak Island mystery treasure will be found.

Four treasures may be hidden on

COCOS ISLAND.

Cocos is a lonely island in the Pacific Ocean. Pirates found it to be a safe hiding place for short periods of time. The island wasn't inhabited by natives as it was a hot, jungle-like place and was not easily located.

Legends say that four different pirate bands buried treasures on the island. Some of the pirates left maps. Others told their children where the treasures were hidden.

In 1844 John Keating found a treasure on Cocos Island. When he died, he told his wife about another one.

Hundreds of people have tried to find the rest of the treasures on Cocos Island. One man searched for many years. But no one has been successful.

Several big earthquakes have hit Cocos Island. That may be the reason no one has ever found the other treasures.

LOST AND FOUND TREASURE TROVES

Today, people are finding treasures that have been lost for centuries. The reason is that today's divers wear oxygen tanks. With these tanks, divers can stay underwater a long time.

Two boys wearing oxygen tanks found an

INDIAN OCEAN TREASURE.

Mark Smith and Bobby Kriegel were living with their parents on the island of Ceylon in 1961. They learned how to dive, using oxygen tanks. While learning to dive underwater with the tanks, they made underwater photographs with Mike Wilson, an ocean explorer.

One day Mike Wilson saw a cannonball in the water. The boys went down to the ocean floor. There they saw a cannon and some silver coins. They had stumbled on the wreck of a treasure ship!

From the wreck, divers brought up many bags of silver coins, cannons, part of a pistol, and a copper plate.

The boys liked finding the sunken wreck. Better yet, they made a movie about finding treasure!

In 1985, a man found the

TREASURE OF THE GHOST GALLEONS.

Mel Fisher is a treasure-hunter who lives in Florida. When he was young, he heard many stories about the lost treasures of the ghost galleons. So he decided to search for them.

He learned that in 1622, twenty-eight Spanish galleons left the New World for the long trip across the Atlantic Ocean. The *Santa Margarita* was one of these ships. It carried a huge treasure of gold and silver. The *Nuestra Senora de Atocha* carried a rich treasure, too.

The galleons were sailing near Florida when the sky turned dark. Hurricane winds pushed the ships into a sandbar. The ships crashed. And powerful waves ripped them to pieces.

Some people from the *Santa Margarita* made it safely to land. They helped their countrymen find the wreck of the ship. But they only found part of its treasure.

Years and years passed by. People lost track of where the *Santa Margarita* wreck lay. And no one had *ever* found the *Atocha*.

For the next 300 years, treasure-hunters searched for the two rich treasure ships. But no one could find them. People began to call them "ghost galleons."

Mel Fisher spent sixteen years looking for these treasure ships. Finally, in 1985, he found the *Atocha*. The next year he found the *Santa Margarita*.

Some people say that the treasures in these ships are the richest ever found.

One of the most sought-after sunken ships of this century has been the

TITANIC.

Found September 1, 1985 by a U.S.-French group, the wreck of the great ship lies, "like an eerie underwater museum," more than two miles down in the North Atlantic. It is 350 miles southeast of Newfoundland.

The discovery was made possible through the aid of Alvin, a 3-man submersible ship, and a robot called Jason Jr.

The once glamorous ship had been thought of as perfect. . . and unsinkable. Yet she had sunk five days into her first voyage in 1912, after striking an iceberg.

Those who found the sunken wreck saw china cups, wine bottles, a doll's head, electric heaters, a silver serving bowl, a brass-and-crystal light fixture, and one of the ship's four safes.

Jason's mechanical arm turned the handle on the safe, but the door would not open. Probably nothing is in the safe anyway, because one of the ship's survivors said that shortly before the ship sank, he saw crew members emptying it.

Many hope that what's left of the mighty *Titanic* will be left to lie in peace. Of the 2,227 people on board the ship, 1,522 drowned. A plaque from the Titanic Historical Society, listing the ship's dead, was placed on the underwater wreck.

You've learned a lot about treasures. You know that some treasures were hidden by pirates. Others were lost when ships sank. Still other treasures are valuable things that are tucked away in safe places.

Some of these treasures show us how people used to live and what they thought was valuable.

What is your greatest treasure?

Is it a piggy bank full of coins? A collection of insects? A box of jewelry?

Whatever your treasure is, you may want to hide it. If you do, be sure to hide it at night when everyone else is asleep. Lock your dog in the basement so he won't know where to dig.

After you have hidden your treasure, draw a map so you can find it again.

When you want your treasure back, wait until it is dark and the moon is not shining. Follow your map, and dig.

Whatever you do, keep quiet! Otherwise, your treasure may vanish right before your eyes.

Index